Appliqué
Borders An Added Grace

Jeana Kimball

CREDITS

Photography . . . . Brent Kane
Illustration and Graphics . . . . Stephanie Benson
Text and Cover Design . . . . Judy Petry
Editor . . . . Liz McGehee

Front Cover: (Top) Double Vine Border, Jeana Kimball, 1990; (Middle) Simple Vine with Bud and Blossom, Marian Baker, 1990; (Bottom) Complex Floral Border, Jeana Kimball, 1988. These vine-type borders show how versatile a vine border treatment can be.

Appliqué Borders: An Added Grace©
©1991 by Jeana Kimball

That Patchwork Place, Inc.
PO Box 118, Bothell, WA 98041-0118

Printed in the Republic of Korea
96 95 94 93 92 91   6 5 4 3 2 1

Library of Congress Cataloging-in-Publication Data

Kimball, Jeana.
    Appliqué borders : an added grace / by Jeana Kimball.
        p.   cm.
    Includes bibliographical references.
    ISBN 0-943574-85-4 :
    1. Appliqué—Patterns. 2. Patchwork—Patterns.
        I. Title.
TT779.K55   1991
746.9'7—dc20
                                        91-17704
                                            CIP

DEDICATION

To my friends and colleagues:

Marian Baker
Maureen Blosch
Annette Bracken
Becky Brown
Minerva Colemere
Elline Craig
Beth Crawford
Kristine Haas
Elna Johnson
Eleanor Tracy
Nancy J. Martin
Joyce Stewart
Shirley Thompson

who shared their time, enthusiasm, and beautiful work
to make this book possible.

CONTENTS

INTRODUCTION

Appliqué borders offer the quiltmaker an opportunity to make a statement about herself, her quilt, and its purpose. Depending on how it is executed and the complexity of its design, an appliqué border can make a quilt formal or spontaneous; it can project a hurried finish or demonstrate its maker's delight in hand appliqué.

Different types of borders suggest different purposes. A swag gives a quilt the illusion of an elegant scalloped finish without having the added difficulty of attaching a binding to the scalloped outside edge. The vine-type border leads the eye around the quilt and back over its surface, thus encouraging one to look longer at a quilt. An appliqué border can also be the unexpected finish that brings a pieced quilt to life. The Ocean Waves quilt on page 20 is an excellent example of how an appliqué border can give a different twist to an old favorite. Whether simple or complex, the border "finishes" the quilt design, while giving the quilt a feeling of continuity and balance.

Because I feel so strongly that appliqué borders make a personal statement and add the finishing touch to quilts, it was clear that a book of appliqué borders would make the designs in my two earlier books, *Reflections of Baltimore* and *Red and Green: An Appliqué Tradition*, complete.

This book includes a pattern for the Ocean Waves quilt shown on page 20, as well as sixteen full-size appliqué border patterns and eighteen border sketches, ranging from simple to complex. These border ideas have been included to help guide you in the design and stitching of your own appliqué borders. The patterns and sketches can be adjusted and adapted to fit any quilt by following the directions on pages 6–8. Should you not find the exact border you need, instructions for designing and drafting your own appliqué border are also included. For basic information on appliquéing, see the Glossary of Techniques beginning on page 28.

PLANNING

Many quiltmakers feel compelled to plan their entire quilt before taking the first stitch. My approach is much more flexible; I plan the number of blocks the quilt will include and then keep an open mind as the blocks are stitched as to what kind of border will enhance them most. When all the blocks are finished, I lay them out next to each other, then stand back and think about the border and what it should include to best enhance the quilt's center. I ask myself the following questions.

Should the border simply frame the quilt's blocks without distracting from the center design?

Does the quilt need an extra something to bring it together and add a spark?

Does it look like the beginning of a masterpiece that needs an elaborate border to finish it properly?

Only you can answer these questions and determine what is right for your quilt. No two people think exactly alike and, therefore, no two people will plan the same border to frame their quilt. Your blocks may suggest a swag, a simple vine, or even a complex floral border.

While deciding which border will best complement your quilt center, consider the following suggestions:

1. A border that incorporates motifs or shapes from the quilt center will coordinate well. Use the full-size or a smaller version of a motif from the center, or a different version with similar characteristics, such as the pineapple used in the border of Annette Bracken's "A Pineapple for Elise" (page 18). Using the same or similar elements in both the quilt center and border gives the quilt design continuity and balance.

2. Repeating the fabrics used in the quilt's center also helps blend the border and quilt together; or, using the same fabric in a different combination can add a new dimension to a quilt. The antique Single Stem Rose Variation quilt on page 146 of *Red and Green: An Appliqué Tradition* is an excellent example of how using new appliqué elements adds a "spark" to an otherwise ordinary group of quilt blocks.

   If you find that you don't have enough fabric to complete the border, this is a perfect place to add a similar fabric in a print or a lighter or darker shade than the original. Using the new fabric along with the original makes it blend well, and its use appears intentional. When this has happened to me, the introduction of a new fabric has enhanced rather than detracted from the design. The Hexagon Rose Wreath quilt shown on page 17 and on the front cover is a good example of the successful use of a new fabric in the border. A green print was used in the border when only solid green fabric was used in the quilt's center.

3. If the center of your quilt is made of Baltimore Album–type or complex floral blocks, consider whether a simple border, such as a swag, would best frame the different quilt blocks and keep the quilt from becoming "busy." Maybe a complex floral border would be more effective in making your quilt a true masterpiece. Look for examples of both kinds of border treatments on pages 17–19.

   When a complex floral border is planned, vary the shape and size of the flowers arranged along the center stem. For example, the use of round pieces (such as cherries), with gently rounded shapes (a rose, for example) and the sharp, pointed edges of the carnation, all add interest to a complex, floral quilt border. The variety makes it more appealing.

4. Time may be a consideration when stitching the quilt border. Complex appliqué borders take much more time to stitch than a swag. Think about the amount of time you have to complete the quilt before choosing or designing a very elaborate border.

   If you find the border design you have chosen is too complicated, simplify it by removing a few leaves or buds. Each leaf you remove can actually eliminate four (one from each side).

5. Although there are many patterns and border ideas here, be conscious of borders and settings on all quilts you see. Make a mental note, as well as a written record, of border designs that you like and would like to adapt in your own work. Keeping a file of border ideas is a good way to help you decide what is best for your quilt.

6. Keep an open mind to what your quilt might be telling you. My friend, Joyce Stewart of Rexburg, Idaho, tells about one of the first quilts she made. She had finished the quilt top, put it into the quilt frame, and was quilting it, when she says, "the quilt spoke to me." I just knew that the border I had used wasn't right; it needed something more. During the quilting, she kept arguing with and assuring herself that it would be okay the way it was. Even after the quilting was completed, she knew it still needed something more. She said the quilt just would not let her bind it, so she started thinking about possible border additions. Luckily, Joyce had left the backing very large so she was able to add two more borders. With the addition of the new borders, the quilt was finally right, so she put it back on the quilt frame, finished quilting, and bound it. All of the debate and extra work was worth the effort because the quilt went on to win Best of Show in a state contest, was featured in the *AQS 1986 Engagement Calendar*, and is to be published in a quilt pattern book. If Joyce had not listened to her quilt and her own judgment, the quilt might not have enjoyed the acclaim it now receives.

   Above all, trust yourself and your own good judgment; if you feel the border is right, it is. Your quilt is your creation, and no one knows it as well as you do.

   There are sixteen full-size border patterns included on the pattern sheets and eighteen sketches of various appliqué borders on pages 24–26. Each sketch is accompanied by a listing of the design's source. The sketches are presented as an aid in planning and designing your own unique version should you choose to do so. The reference allows you to go to the original source to closely examine the complete quilt for further ideas on color and block arrangement. If you don't find a border here to suit you or your quilt, design your own border. Elements from borders given here can be incorporated into your original border design. Border design is not difficult; just follow the instructions in the next section, which explains how to construct a master pattern.

CONSTRUCTION

A master pattern is needed for every quilt's border, even if the repeats are exactly right to fit the border patterns given here. Every quilt is unique in size and appearance, even if it is a duplicate of a particular pattern. The master pattern is used to trace the border onto your fabric for appliqué placement and as a reference while you stitch. The Individual Border Instructions (pages 10–16) specify the size of the repeated element in the border. Measurements for finished borders are not given, since all quilts will vary in size, depending on the number of quilt blocks and the width of the border. The borders presented in this book are easily adjusted when making the master pattern, following the step-by-step directions.

Master Pattern

Read *all* instructions for making a master pattern for the border you have chosen *before* beginning to work. Once you understand the steps needed for your border, you are ready to begin.

If your quilt will have the same size border repeats as the patterns given here, follow steps 1–3 and then proceed to Making Templates on page 8.

Should you choose to adapt or adjust the size of a vine-type border from the pattern section, follow steps 1, 2, 4, and 5.

To design a vine-type border, including complex floral designs, follow steps 1, 2, 4, and 6.

For adjusting or designing a swag border, follow steps 1, 2, 7, 8, and 9.

1. Use butcher paper or smaller sheets of paper taped together to make a paper pattern that equals one-quarter or one-half of the quilt's finished border. (See illustrations below.) Step 2 explains whether a master pattern with one-quarter or one-half section is needed for vine-type borders. All swag borders use a master pattern with a one-quarter section.

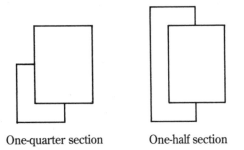

One-quarter section   One-half section

When planning how wide the border should be, make the border half the width of the individual quilt blocks, plus one or two inches. For example, a quilt with 16" blocks would generally have a border that is 10" wide ($16'' \div 2 = 8'' + 2'' = 10''$). This formula for determining the border width produces a border that blends well and balances with the quilt's center. However, if you would like to emphasize the border as a focal point of the quilt, a wider border is more appropriate. If the border is to be simple and a minimal part of the intended overall effect of the quilt, a narrower border is best.

2. Fold the paper pattern into equal sections. The folds will divide the master pattern into sections that will be proportionately filled with border design.

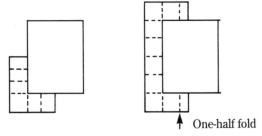

↑ One-half fold

There are two kinds of vine-type borders:

Type A: a vine that fills each quarter section of the border equally but does not necessarily flow continuously around the quilt;

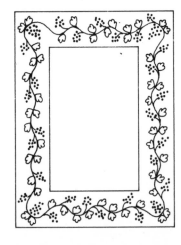

Type B: a vine that travels all the way around the perimeter of the quilt without a break and with all appliqué elements traveling in one direction.

Type A borders require a master pattern that is a one-quarter section of the finished border. (See illustration under step 1 [left].) Square quilts usually require a Type A border.

Type B borders require a master pattern that is a one-half section of the finished border. (See illustration under step 1 [right].) On the width side, the last folded section is a one-half section (See arrows on illustration under step 2 [right].) Care should be taken while folding the master pattern to make this last section a partial fold. The partial section allows the border to flow continuously without interruption.

3. Trace the border from your chosen pattern pages.

4. If you have chosen to design or need to adjust a vine-type border, draw a line through the center of the length of the master pattern. Next, draw a vine that flows evenly through the divided sections.

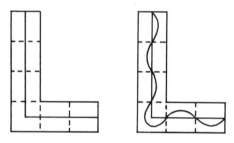

5. Next, transfer the appliqué motifs from the pattern section onto your master pattern in the arrangement shown, using the divided border sections as a guide to how each should fit along the vine. If the flower and leaf shapes are too large or too small, use a photocopy machine to reduce or enlarge (by 5% or 10% increments) the motifs to the appropriate size for your border. Then trace the new pattern pieces onto the master pattern.

6. When designing a vine-type border, arrange the flowers and leaves along the vine, using a consistent number of flowers and leaves in each section. I like to work with paper pattern pieces when designing because they are easy to cut, fold, and adjust. See Making Pattern Pieces on page 28 in the Glossary of Techniques.

Complex floral borders can incorporate secondary branches to help "fill out" the border. Complex floral borders should include a variety of shapes and sizes in both flowers and leaves.

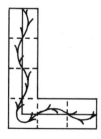

7. If you have chosen to design a swag, begin with one of the full-size swag pieces on one of the pattern sheets to get you started and help set the curve. When designing swags, I like to work with paper pattern pieces because they are easy to cut, fold, and adjust.

8. For a swag border, make a swag piece that will fit between fold lines to fill each section. If possible, all folded side sections of the master pattern should be the same size so that one swag template can be used around the entire border. If it is not possible to make all the folded side sections exactly the same size, make the corner section larger. Adjustments can be made to the corner swag piece by enlarging or reducing its size or placement to compensate for the uneven measurement.

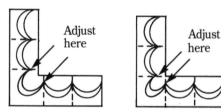

Adjust the size of the swag piece to make it fit the sections of your master pattern as follows:

To enlarge a swag, cut it through the center, spread the two halves until the swag is the correct size, then tape the swag pieces together with a filler piece in the center.

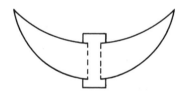

To reduce a swag piece, fold it in the center and then adjust the folded edge to make swag piece smaller. Adjust the fold so that a slightly larger section is taken from the bottom of the swag than from the top of the swag piece.

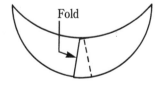

9. Make the corner swag piece last. Taking the swag used for side sections, fold it so that a large section is removed from the top center of the swag.

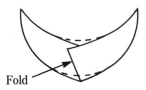

Fold

In the illustration on the right below, the swags are placed closer to the quilt center than in the illustration on the left. By placing the swags closer to or farther from the quilt center, adjustments can be made to use a large or small corner swag piece.

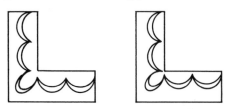

Making Templates

Using plastic template material, trace and cut each template pattern piece the actual size, as it appears on the master pattern. If a pattern piece will be used only a few times in constructing the border, you can use paper templates instead. To make paper templates the easy way, photocopy your master pattern and cut it apart into individual pattern pieces.

Fabric Selection

Appliqué is most successful when 100% cotton fabric is used. Cotton is easier to turn under and stays in place more readily than synthetic fabrics. To add visual interest and texture, use a combination of solids and prints.

Marking and Cutting

Before beginning to stitch the first border section, mark, cut out, pin, and arrange your fabric pieces on a separate piece of paper or fabric (apart from your background fabric). This "pin-up" gives you the option to change your mind and rearrange colors or fabrics, so that the final product will please you. The pin-up is especially important for a complex floral border.

Each appliqué piece is marked on the right side of the fabric for needle-turn appliqué. See the Glossary of Techniques on pages 29–31 for a description of needle-turn appliqué. Mark each piece by accurately tracing around the template. A mechanical pencil is preferred for mark-

ing because it gives a sharp, accurate line. On dark fabric, a silver- or yellow-colored pencil is recommended.

Using a sharp pair of scissors, cut out each piece ³⁄₁₆" from the marked pencil line. A wider seam allowance causes lumpy edges, while a narrower one frays easily.

Cutting and Attaching Background Fabric Borders

Cut out and attach the four border strips as follows:

1. Measure the width and length of the quilt center by measuring across the center of the quilt top. Measurements taken along the edge are not accurate since the sides are not as stable as the center of the quilt.
2. Determine desired border width (page 6) and add an extra 1½"–2". Any excess border can be trimmed from the outer edge later.
3. I find it helpful to sketch the quilt plus the border when calculating how long to cut border strips for each side of the quilt, adding an extra 1" at each end to allow for seam allowances.

A = quilt length
B = quilt width
C = border width

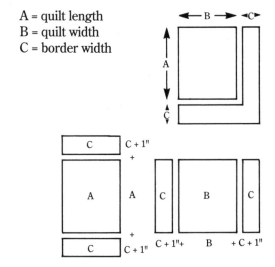

4. To attach borders:
   a. Fold border strip in half crosswise and finger press the center point of edge that will be attached to the quilt top.
   b. Fold coordinating side of quilt top in half and finger press center point.
   c. Match the two finger-pressed folds and pin with right sides together.
   d. Working from the center out, carefully pin the rest of the border to the quilt top, making sure that an equal length of border extends beyond quilt center on both sides.
   e. Using a ¼"-wide seam allowance, stitch border strip to quilt top from seam allowance to seam allowance.
   f. Repeat for remaining three borders.

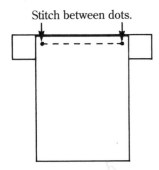

Stitch between dots.

5. To miter border corners:
  a. Fold quilt in half diagonally so the two borders of the corner you are mitering are parallel.

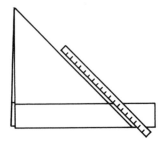

Wrong side of quilt

Pin to stablilize borders while you are marking and stitching.
  b. Use one of two methods to mark stitching line for mitered corner:
    (1) Place a yardstick along the diagonal fold and mark a pencil line on border along yardstick.

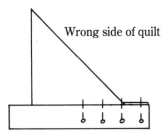

    (2) Use a 90° right-angle template (purchased from an art supply store or made by cutting a perfect square in half) to mark the stitching line. Place point of right angle on last stitch in corner of quilt body. Line up straight side of template with the stitching that attaches borders to body of quilt. Draw stitching line along diagonal side of template.

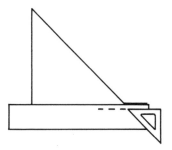

  c. Pin and stitch along pencil line.
  d. Press seam that attached border to quilt center toward quilt center. Once assured that miter is accurate, trim away excess border fabric and press remaining seam allowance open or to one side, whichever you prefer.

Transferring the Master Pattern

The master pattern will fit one-fourth (if a Type A Border) or one-half (if a Type B Border) the size of the finished border. Arrange the master pattern under the background fabric border. Line up the inside edge of the master pattern with the seam joining the border to the quilt center, making sure that the corner lines up first. The master pattern is now lined up with the background fabric; pin. To mark the background fabric for placement of appliqué pieces, trace lightly ¼" inside the design.

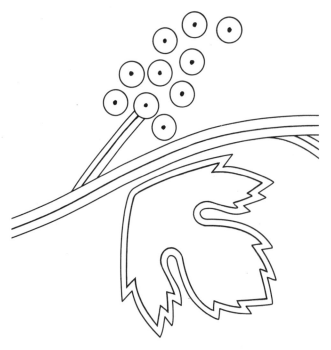

For stems, mark one line through the center of the stem, not two lines on either side. By marking ¼" inside actual placement, you allow extra room for shifting as appliqué progresses, and you keep the placement marking for the appliqué hidden.

Appliqué Tips

Appliqué pieces are stitched onto background fabric the way a plant grows: first the stem, next the leaves and buds, and finally the flowers. Follow this general rule when determining the order in which to appliqué the pieces. Refer to the master pattern while appliquéing to ensure correct order of placement.

For basic appliqué how-tos, see the Glossary of Techniques on pages 28–34.

INDIVIDUAL BORDER INSTRUCTIONS

SIMPLE SWAG

(See photo of border on the inside front cover.)

This swag is a versatile pattern. Because of the even width along its body, it is easily adjusted for size without distorting its shape. The swag piece shown is 8" from point to point, and the border background fabric is 10" wide. Notice that there is no corner swag piece used in this border; the swag pieces simply meet in the corner. The triple leaves where the points meet can be replaced with elements from your quilt to make the swag "tie in" with your quilt design.

SWAG WITH INVERTED DETAIL

(See photo of border on the inside front cover.)

Most swag borders are embellished with detail at the uppermost point where the swag ends meet. This interesting variation features detail under the points instead. Elline Craig designed this border from an antique quilt she saw in a local historic home. The swag piece measures 10" from point to point, and the border background fabric is 10" wide. Time is saved when appliquéing this border, since the bud is appliquéd in place along one side only. The remaining raw edges are concealed when the swag pieces are appliquéd over the bud.

Double Swag from Asymmetrical Rose Quilt

(See photo of full quilt on page 18.)

Beth Crawford used the double swag to frame her four-block quilt and embellished the border swags with the addition of a yellow teardrop-shaped bud inside the dark red swag section. The finished border background fabric is 10" wide, and the swag measures 9" from point to point. The corner leaf additions on the pattern sheet can be added if the corner of your quilt needs more substance to balance the quilt.

Double Swag from Red and Green Garden

(See photo of full quilt on the inside front cover.)

Eleanor Tracy used a simple border treatment to surround the varied patterns of the block collection. A complex floral border may have made the quilt "busy," but the red and green swag was just right to pull the design together. The border background fabric is 10" wide, and the swag measures 9" from point to point.

Simple Vine with Bud and Blossom

(See photo of border on the front cover.)

Alternating buds and blossoms combine in this appealing border designed by Marian Baker. Marian's Whig Rose Variation quilt is effectively framed with buds and blossoms like those in its quilt blocks. This border pattern has been altered slightly from the one shown to make it more symmetrical as the vine flows around the corner. To personalize this Type B border to fit your quilt, substitute elements from your quilt blocks. The finished width of the border is 10". Each folded section on the master pattern is 11" wide, with the vine rotating across the center line at the folded sections. With all of the buds on the outside edge and the flowers on the inside edge, the same elements are only repeated at 22" intervals.

Double Scalloped Swag from Bride of Tulip Valley

(See photo of full quilt on page 19.)

Two layers of scallops combine to make this feminine swag border. The scalloped outside edge makes adjusting the size a little more difficult. The swag pattern is 9" from point to point, and the border background fabric is 8" wide. When stitching this border, the lower swag piece does not need to be appliquéd where it is covered by the top swag piece. However, be careful to cut fabric for this lower swag piece so that it extends well under the scallops of the top layer. That way, no raw edges will be exposed accidentally.

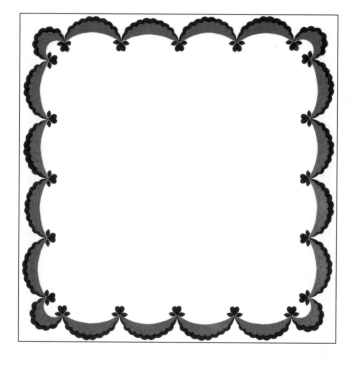

SIMPLE VINE WITH SINGLE FLOWER

(See photo of full quilt on page 19.)

This simple vine border is used on a wall quilt to surround one appliqué block. Its design was adapted from a quilting pattern by Shirley Thompson in her book, *It's Not a Quilt Until It's Quilted*. This border is designed as a Type A border but could easily be adapted as a Type B border. The design repeats every 4" from flower to flower, with the stem adjusted up or down with each repeat.

BUDS AND BLOSSOM VINE BORDER

(See photo of full quilt on the inside back cover.)

This Type A border was designed by Maureen Blosch to frame a single appliqué quilt block. The number of vine rotations between the border center point and corners can be increased to enlarge this design. The finished border is 8½" wide with a 15" repeat from the center of the corner to the border center.

OAK LEAF AND BUTTERFLIES VINE BORDER

(See photo of full quilt on page 18.)

This border was designed for Elna Johnson's quilt, *Gifts from Nature*, featuring four Oak Leaf blocks. The vine flows around each of the four blocks separately, creating a secondary leaf shape with the trailing vine. The appliqué blocks are 16" square with a 4"-wide inside sashing strip and an 8"-wide outer border. This is a Type A border.

DOUBLE VINE BORDER

(See photo of full quilt on page 17.)

Since this border finishes the square Hexagon Rose Wreath quilt, a Type A border was used. To adapt this border to a rectangular quilt, a Type B master pattern is required. The double vine border has a 10" finished width; however, if dogtooth borders are added, as they were in the Hexagon Rose Wreath quilt, an extra 1¼" in width must be added to the background fabric. There is a 12½" repeat along the vine.

PINEAPPLE/CARNATION VINE BORDER

(See photo of full quilt on page 18.)

Annette Bracken designed a small pineapple motif for her border to bring the focal point of the quilt center to its outside edges. This is a Type B border with a finished width of 10". There is a 10½" repeat along the vine.

PRAIRIE FLOWER VINE BORDER

(See photo of full quilt on page 19.)

Appliqué blocks set on point are effectively framed with this Type A border that fills the half and quarter blocks of the quilt-block setting. A 3"-wide border strip is all that is needed since the majority of the border fills in empty places in the block setting. There is a 21" repeat between the corner and the center fill-in block.

GRAPEVINE BORDER

(See photo of full quilt on page 20.)

During a visit to a glorious antique quilt show, where cameras were not allowed, I made notes on some of the quilts that I especially liked. While recently going over my notes, I noticed an entry, "Ocean Waves Quilt with Grapevine Border," with nothing more about the quilt. I was puzzled; why the single entry with no more detail? Then I realized that it was the combination of Ocean Waves with the grapevine border that I wanted to remember, and not necessarily that quilt. So based on that idea, which was first used in the nineteenth century, I designed this grapevine border to surround an Ocean Waves quilt center. The leaves are from rubbings of my father's grapevines at the house where I grew up. You may want to substitute a variety from your own garden.

The finished border is 12" wide with a repeat of 19" from double set of leaves to double set of leaves. This is a Type B border, since the vine flows in one direction all around the quilt.

DISJOINTED BORDER

(See photo of full quilt on page 18 and a close-up of the border on the inside back cover.)

Sometimes turning the corner on an appliqué border is just too much trouble, and a quiltmaker may want to avoid the corner altogether. In that case, a disjointed border is the perfect solution, since the corners are intentionally left open. This border was designed for the Grace's Quail quilt by Kristine Haas, and it incorporates elements from the Cockscomb in Basket with Birds blocks in the quilt center. The same idea can be adapted to your quilt border by using elements from your quilt blocks in place of the cockscomb flowers. This border is 10" wide.

COMPLEX FLORAL BORDER

(See photo of full quilt on page 17.)

This complex floral border was designed to include appliqué elements from the four different complex floral blocks it frames. All of the appliqué motifs in the border are found in one of the center blocks. You may want to substitute elements from your quilt center on this border. This Type A border looks like a Type B border because the vine seems to continue around the quilt without interruption. However, strategically placed flowers and leaves along the vine conceal the breaks in the vine. The finished border is 9" wide with no repeats of design in each one-fourth border section.

COMPLEX FLORAL SWAG BORDER

(See photo of border on the inside back cover.)

Using appliqué elements from all thirteen of the complex floral blocks in *Reflections of Baltimore*, I designed this complex floral swag to complement any grouping of blocks from the book. The swag section is 16" from point to point and will fit equally around a quilt with 16" finished blocks. The finished border is 10" wide. Colors and fabrics used in the flowers and leaves can be varied with each swag to add contrast to the border. This border can easily be enlarged by "spreading out" the design elements to fit a larger swag area.

GALLERY

Patterns for the appliqué block designs in the quilts pictured here appear in *Red and Green: An Appliqué Tradition*, unless otherwise noted.

Complex Floral Border from Baltimore Beginnings quilt by Jeana Kimball, 1988. Motifs from the blocks in the quilt's center are repeated throughout the border. Repeating these motifs ensures that the border will coordinate with the quilt center. Quilt block patterns appear in Reflections of Baltimore.

Double Vine Border from Hexagon Rose Wreath quilt by Jeana Kimball, 1990. The double-vine border treatment is an unusual vine arrangement that adds just the right finish to this traditional rose-wreath theme.

Oak Leaf and Butterflies Vine Border from Gifts from Nature quilt by Elna Johnson, 1990. The four Oak Leaf blocks are traced with a vine that forms four secondary leaf shapes.

Pineapple/Carnation Vine Border from Pineapple for Elise quilt by Annette Bracken, 1990. The reduced size of the pineapple motif from the quilt center allows the pineapple to be repeated in the border without overwhelming the other border motifs.

Double Swag Border from Asymmetrical Rose quilt by Beth Crawford, 1990. This double swag with tassels adds an elegant finish to the asymmetrical quilt-block design.

Disjointed Border from Grace's Quail quilt by Kristine Haas, 1990. A disjointed border frees one of the need to turn the corner of a border. This border repeats the motifs from the quilt's center but alters the basket to add a new dimension to the border.

Simple Vine with Single Flower Border from Sampler Basket quilt by Jeana Kimball, 1988. The busy center block is calmed with the addition of a simple vine border. The vine finishes the quilt without detracting from the center basket. Quilt block pattern appears in Reflections of Baltimore.

Prairie Flower Vine Border from Victorian Rose quilt by Minerva Colemere, 1990. This border effectively fills in the one-half and quarter blocks that were used to square the "on-point" setting of the blocks.

Double Scalloped Swag from Bride of Tulip Valley quilt by Jeana Kimball, 1987. The scalloped swag adds a lacy finish to this feminine quilt.

Ocean Waves with Grapevine Border, by Jeana Kimball, 1991. Pieced quilts combine very nicely with appliqué borders. As shown here, an appliqué border can "dress up" a quilt center. Fabrics from the quilt center are repeated in the border to give the quilt continuity.

DIRECTIONS FOR OCEAN WAVES QUILT

Templates on page 23

This quilt was stitched using methods described in *Ocean Waves* by Nancy J. Martin and Marsha McCloskey. There are twelve major blocks in the quilt with four single-square block sections making up one quilt block. Each major block is 16" square, and the final dimension is 72" x 92" with the addition of a 12" border all around the Ocean Waves center.

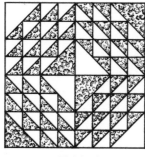

16" block

Materials: 44"-wide fabric
1½" yds. major print (black in quilt shown)
2 yds. various coordinating fabrics
5 yds. background fabric

Cutting
Templates and measurements for Template -Free™ cutting include ¼" seam allowances.

Template Method
Using Template #3, cut 24 triangles from the background fabric and 24 triangles from the major print.

Using Template #1, cut 576 triangles from background fabric and 24 triangles from the coordinating fabrics, or use the Bias Square® Method, below.

Bias-Square Method
Cut 2½"-wide bias strips from ½-yard lengths of background and various coordinating fabrics. Stitch strips together as shown. You will need 14 sets of strips to make 480 bias-square units, each measuring 2½" x 2½" (Template 2).

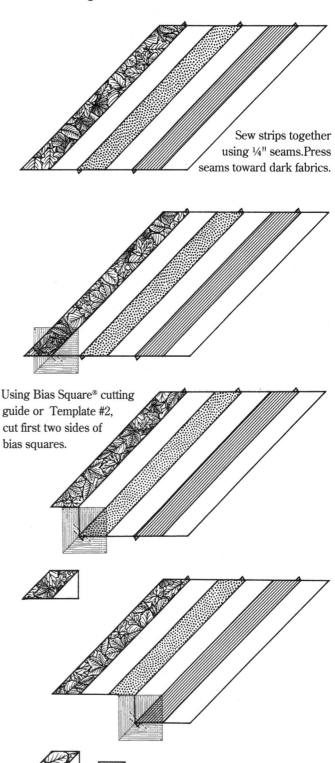

Sew strips together using ¼" seams. Press seams toward dark fabrics.

Using Bias Square® cutting guide or Template #2, cut first two sides of bias squares.

Ocean Waves Quilt Diagram

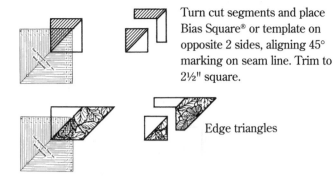

Turn cut segments and place Bias Square® or template on opposite 2 sides, aligning 45° marking on seam line. Trim to 2½" square.

Edge triangles

Resize edge triangles using Template #1. You will need a total of 96 triangles cut from the background fabric and 96 triangles cut from the coordinating fabric.

Directions

1. Piece 48 Ocean Waves blocks as shown. Join blocks in groups of four.

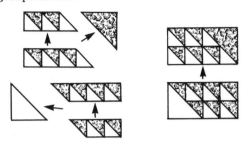

2. Set blocks together in rows. Make four rows, each containing three blocks.
3. Join rows of blocks into a quilt top.
4. Stitch appliqué border, using the Grapevine Border, page 15. Make the border 12" to 13" wide and miter as described on page 9.
5. Add batting and backing, then quilt or tie as desired and finish by binding the outer edges.

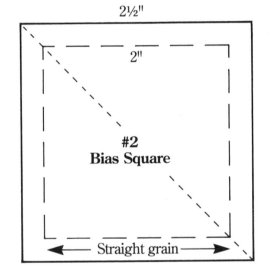

2½"

2"

**#2
Bias Square**

← Straight grain →

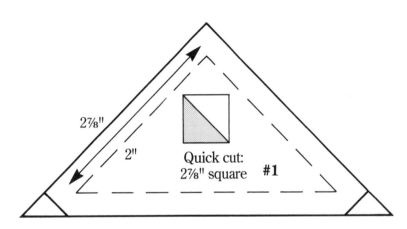

2⅞"

2"

Quick cut:
2⅞" square **#1**

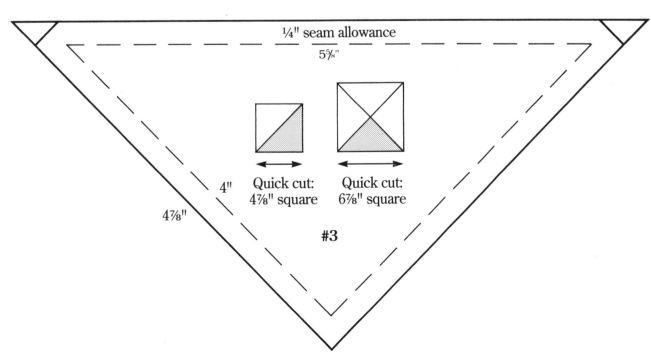

¼" seam allowance

5⅝"

4"

4⅞"

Quick cut:
4⅞" square

Quick cut:
6⅞" square

#3

BORDER SKETCHES

Barbara Brackman, *American Patchwork Quilt,* plate 10.

Carleton Safford and Robert Bishop, *America's Quilts & Coverlets,* page 169.

1984 Quilt Engagement Calendar, plate 9.

Bettina Havig, *Missouri Heritage Quilts,* pages 34–35.

Karoline Patterson Bresenhan and Nancy O'Bryant Puentes, *Lone Stars: A Legacy of Texas Quilts*, 1836–1936, pages 32–33.

Robert Bishop, *Quilts, Coverlets, Rugs & Samplers*, plate 162.

Marsha McDowell and Ruth D. Fitzgerald, *Michigan Quilts: 150 Years of a Textile Tradition*, page 103.

Carleton Safford and Robert Bishop, *America's Quilts & Coverlets*, page 162.

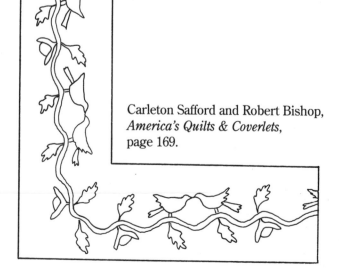

Carleton Safford and Robert Bishop, *America's Quilts & Coverlets*, page 169.

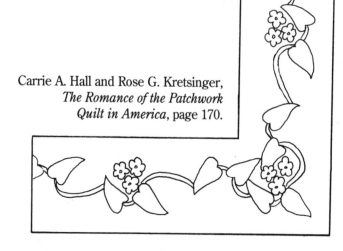

Carrie A. Hall and Rose G. Kretsinger, *The Romance of the Patchwork Quilt in America*, page 170.

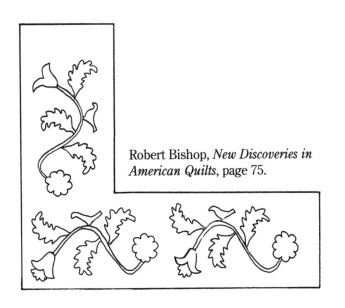

Robert Bishop, *New Discoveries in American Quilts*, page 75.

1982 Quilt Engagement Calendar, plate 32.

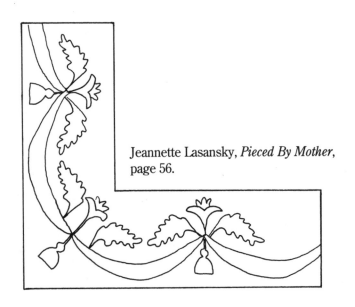

Jeannette Lasansky, *Pieced By Mother,* page 56.

Carleton Safford and Robert Bishop, *America's Quilts & Coverlets,* page 184

Sandi Fox, *Small Endearments*, plate 43.

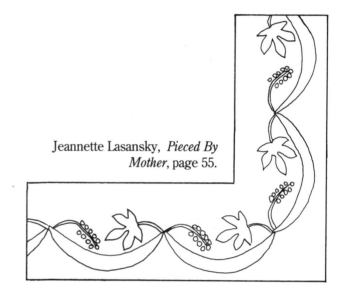

Jeannette Lasansky, *Pieced By Mother*, page 55.

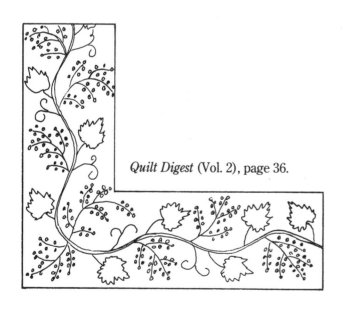

Quilt Digest (Vol. 2), page 36.

Marsha McDowell and Ruth D. Fitzgerald, *Michigan Quilts: 150 Years of a Textile Tradition*, page 21.

GLOSSARY OF TECHNIQUES

MAKING PATTERN PIECES

When designing your own appliqué border or adding or modifying design elements to an existing design, you may find it easier to cut paper shapes than to sketch. You can cut much smoother lines and curves with scissors than you can draw with a pencil. Use a small pair of scissors that fits comfortably in your hand, such as 5" craft scissors. Larger scissors are bulky and more difficult to handle when cutting small paper shapes.

Following are instructions for cutting out three basic "rose" motifs, which are often the foundation for the majority of flowers found in appliqué designs.

Begin with several 3" paper circles. With your compass set at 1½", draw several circles and cut them out. Since your rose may need to be larger or smaller than 3" across, adjust the size of the circle accordingly, making it ¼" to ½" larger than the desired finished size. This allows for trimming and shaping the "petals." Using the paper circles, fold and cut as illustrated to make the desired number of scalloped petals on your flower.

Eight-petal

Eight-Petal Flower

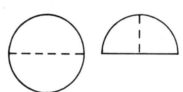

Measure and mark equal distance on each side.　　Cut rounded shape.

Refold and recut as necessary to make petal definition suitable.

Six-Petal Flower

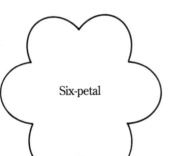

Six-petal

Divide and fold into three equal sections.　　Measure and mark equal distance on each side.　　Cut rounded shape.

Refold and recut as necessary to make petal definition suitable.

Five-Petal Flower

Five-petal

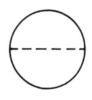

Fold in three divisions as shown.

For ten-petal flower, fold one more time through center.　　Measure and mark equal distance on each side.　　Cut rounded shape.

If you want pointed petals, cut straight lines in the place of rounded ones.

Cut straight lines
for pointed petals

Leaves and buds are easily shaped by cutting a mirror image with just one paper fold. Sketch the basic shape of the motif and then cut out, smoothing and reshaping with the scissors as needed.

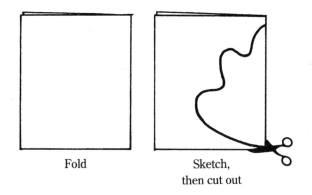

Fold	Sketch, then cut out

If the cutout design is not quite right:

1. Fold another piece of paper in half.
2. Lightly trace half of the previous design onto it.
3. Sketch a new design, correcting and improving the original design lines as desired.
4. Cut out along the new lines.

Repeat the previous steps as many times as necessary until you're pleased with the shape of the design motif.

If the cutout motif is the exact shape you need, but not the right size, enlarge or reduce it several times on a photocopy machine. Leave the copy machine cover open so that the shapes are well defined against a black background. Adjust the reduction or enlargement in 5% to 10% increments each time. One of the several sizes you try is sure to fit your needs perfectly.

NEEDLE-TURN APPLIQUÉ

The needle-turn method of appliqué is one in which the needle is used as a tool to turn under the raw edge of the fabric as you stitch. This method provides a smooth, clean edge, and, with a little practice, becomes quick and easy to use. The need for time-consuming basting is completely eliminated, but a little extra care is needed to make sure the appliqué pieces are positioned correctly before beginning to stitch.

The needle is an important part of this method. A long, fine needle is highly recommended. I prefer size 11 Sharps or size 10 straw needles.

1. Cut an 18" length of thread in a color that matches the appliqué piece. If the thread is too long, it tends to knot and tangle. Cut thread at an angle to assist in threading it into the small eye of the needle.
2. Tie a knot in the end of the thread. To make a small, firm knot that will not come undone, hold the threaded needle in your right hand, between thumb and forefinger, and the tail of the thread in your left hand, pointing them toward each other.

Grasp the end of the thread in the fingers holding the needle, and use the left hand to wrap the thread around the needle four or five times. Hold the wraps with the right thumb and forefinger and pull the needle through the wraps with the left hand. Hold the wraps tightly until the thread is pulled all the way through. You will have a small, firm knot, similar to a French knot. Cut off any excess thread tail.

3. Position the appliqué piece on the spot where it is to be sewn by putting a pin through the point where it should touch an adjoining piece. For example, it is best to first pin a leaf through the point where it will touch the stem.

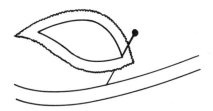

This is important, since the raw edges have not yet been turned under, and it is difficult to determine the exact placement. Pin in place with an adequate number of pins, but don't pin too heavily as the pins might get in the way and catch the thread during stitching. For example, a simple, small leaf requires two pins.

4. It is important to begin stitching on the straightest edge possible and as close as possible to the point where the piece being appliquéd touches an adjoining appliqué piece.

If you are right-handed, stitch counterclockwise; if you are left-handed, stitch clockwise. Begin by using the threaded needle to catch and turn under the seam allowance that has been marked on the right side of the fabric. Once the seam allowance is turned under, use the left thumbnail (or tip of thumb) on the top and the second finger of the left hand underneath the fabric as a clamp to hold the turned-under seam allowance in place as you stitch. This helps ensure a smooth edge.

Take the first stitch by bringing the needle up through the background fabric, through the seam allowance that has been turned under, and out through the fold of the piece being appliquéd.

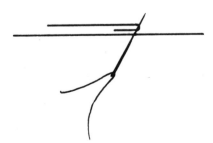

Make the next stitch by inserting the needle into the background fabric only, immediately next to the first stitch. (The tip of the needle is now touching your fingers underneath the piece.) Turn the needle horizontally, travel along approximately 1/16" on the wrong side of the background fabric, and then bring the needle straight up, through the background fabric and through the fold as before.

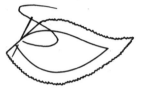

Do not slant the needle when going in or out of the fabric, or the appliquéd edge will not lie flat and the stitches may show on the top. Stitches should be invisible on top; only slight indentations, where stitches have been taken, should be visible. As each stitch is completed, give a little "tug" on the thread. This will anchor the appliqué to the background, firmly joining them together.

Continue stitching this way, spacing the stitches approximately 1/16" apart. The wrong side of the background fabric should show even spans of thread, with only a tiny gap where the thread has gone through to the top to take a "bite" out of the fold.

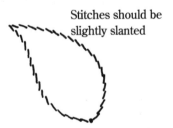

Stitches should be slightly slanted

Two problem spots that are often encountered in appliqué are making sharp points and keeping inverted points from fraying. Use the following techniques to eliminate these problems.

Making Sharp Points. Stitch in the method described earlier, along the edge of the piece and right up to the point of the piece, taking the last stitch in the pencil-marked point.

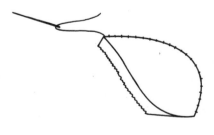

Turn the entire block so the stitching will progress in the proper direction (counterclockwise for right-handed, clockwise for left-handed). Using fine, sharp scissors, trim the excess seam allowance away; then, using the needle as a tool, begin at the point and turn and tuck under the seam allowance. If the point of the piece gets pushed under in the process of turning the seam allowance, give a little tug on the thread and the point will pop back out into place. After the seam allowance has been turned under satisfactorily, take the next stitch going away from the point and proceed as usual.

The secret to making perfect, sharp points is to be sure the excess fabric has been trimmed before turning under the seam allowance. Remember, all the excess fabric has to fit under that tiny point and if there is too much, the point will be round and lumpy.

Fray-Free Inverted Points. Before pinning the appliqué piece to the background fabric, clip through the seam allowance to the pencil-marked point, making sure to clip all the way to the pencil line.

Clip

As you stitch toward the inverted point, such as the center of a heart, take the appliqué stitches closer together. Two stitches from the point, turn the whole quilt block so that the stitching will progress in the proper direction after the point is stitched.

In preparation for taking the next few stitches, turn under the seam allowance on the other side of the inverted point.

Next, using the needle as a tool, smooth under with a sweeping motion any stray threads that may be protruding from the inverted point. The needle will move be-

tween the background fabric and the appliqué piece to make the "sweep."

When satisfied that all stray threads are tucked under, take the next stitch or two toward the point. The center stitch (in the point) is made by taking a deep stitch. On all other appliqué stitches, only a small "bite" is taken from the edge of the fold. This stitch is made by bringing the needle up several threads (4 to 5 threads) inside the point. Continue the stitch, placing the point of the needle underneath the edge of the appliqué motif (with needle point out of view) and enter the background fabric, right next to where the needle came up for the deep stitch.

Finish the stitch by moving the needle horizontally underneath the background fabric to take the next stitch and proceed as usual.

This deep stitch creates a tuck that pulls all of the fraying threads down and under and holds them in place.

CUTTING AWAY THE FABRIC BEHIND THE APPLIQUÉ

Cutting away the background fabric will make a big difference in the finished work. It will make the appliqué lie flatter and eliminate the possibility of having to quilt through extra layers of fabric. Separate the appliqué from the background fabric, then make a snip in the background fabric just large enough to slide the scissors inside. Trim away the background fabric ¼" inside the appliqué stitches. Do not cut away background fabric behind very small appliqué pieces or stems.

Do not cut away the background fabric until you are certain the appliqué piece is positioned correctly. When several layers of appliqué are used, cut away each background layer before appliquéing the next.

PERFECT CIRCLE CONSTRUCTION

Circles are a challenge in appliqué because it is difficult to begin and end stitching on a curve while keeping the curve smooth. This method was developed to assist in keeping all edges smooth and round.

1. Make a stiff plastic template the actual size of the finished circle. This template is used in the stitching of the circle. The finished product is dependent on the shape of the plastic template, so it is extremely important that the template be a perfect circle. It is helpful to use a circle template which can be purchased at an office supply store.
2. Make a second template for cutting the fabric circle, making it twice as big as the actual-size circle template. For example, a ½"-diameter circle requires a 1"-diameter circle cut from fabric.
3. Using matching thread that has been knotted, baste ⅛" from the raw edges around the fabric circle. After basting is completed, place the plastic template on the wrong side of the circle and draw up the thread to encase the template inside the fabric.
4. Without tying a knot or cutting the thread, stitch back and forth across the circle through the gathers, as if making the spokes of a wagon wheel. Cut thread; a knot at this stage is not necessary. The last step will hold the turned edge in place until appliqué is complete.

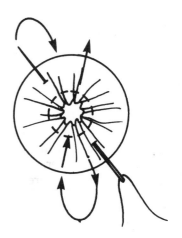

Note: This step pulls any possible bumps or peaks away from the outside edge, leaving a perfectly round, smooth edge to stitch down. The plastic template will be removed in the last step.

5. Position the prepared circle in its proper location on the background fabric and hold firmly in place while appliquéing, using small stitches. Be sure to take the stitches on the edge of the circle only, catching a few threads with each stitch. After the circle is stitched into place, tie a knot on the wrong side of the background fabric.
6. On the wrong side, use a small scissors with strong, sharp points to carefully pierce and cut down through the background fabric and excess gathered fabric, until it touches the plastic template. Cut out a small circle, removing excess gathered fabric. Leave at least ⅛" allowance of fabric to prevent fraying. Remove the plastic template by sliding it out, as if unbuttoning a button. The plastic template can be reused for the remaining circles in the design.

To make padded or stuffed cherries, place a very small amount of stuffing inside the basted fabric circle before adding the plastic template. When the template is removed, the stuffing stays in place under the edges of the ⅛" allowance left after trimming away the background. Crisscross stitches may be taken to form a web that holds the stuffing in, but care must be taken to make these stitches loose since the cherry can be distorted if the stitches are pulled tight.

ALTERNATE PERFECT CIRCLE METHOD

Some of the circles in appliqué patterns are used as flower centers, or they overlap previous appliqué stitching lines. When this occurs, use the following circle construction method:

1. Follow Steps 1 through 3 for the perfect circle construction technique, with the exception of using the plastic template. Instead, cut the template from cardboard, such as a manila folder.
2. After drawing up the basting thread, tie a knot and cut the thread.
3. Press the circle firmly with a hot iron.
4. Remove the basting thread and the cardboard template.
5. Trim excess fabric as necessary and appliqué into place along the pressed edge.

BIAS-STRIP CONSTRUCTION

Bias strips in appliquéd borders are usually ⅜" to ½" wide. For ⅜"-wide finished bias strips, cut strips 1¼" wide. For ½"-wide finished bias strips, cut strips 1½" wide.

1. Cut the strips to the desired width and the required length, cutting on the true bias of the fabric.
2. Fold the strip in half lengthwise, wrong sides together, and hand or machine baste the raw edges together, using a scant ¼"-wide seam allowance.
3. Press the bias strip flat, making sure the seam allowance is pressed to the underside of the strip. The seam allowance will be hidden under the bias strip when it is stitched down.

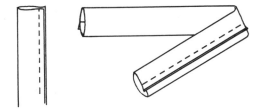

PROPORTIONAL PETAL SPACING

This technique was devised to help in planning the placement of identical petals on a multi-petaled flower, so that the distance between petals is equal. Without this technique, some of the petals on a four-petal flower, for example, might overlap too much while others might leave a large gap. Use this method for the flowers in the Simple Vine with Single Flower Border shown on page 13.

1. Make a template for a single petal, adding a small notch on each side of the petal where it will overlap

the one next to it, as shown. The notches will be used in positioning the second and all succeeding petals.

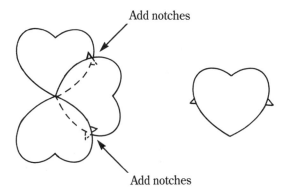

2. On the right side of the background fabric, trace the required number of petals for each flower, being sure to mark the notches.
3. Appliqué the first petal, following the normal appliqué steps and ignoring the notches.
4. Position the next petal by placing a pin through the pencil-marked point and into the point of the finished petal.

Rotate the second petal alongside the appliquéd petal until the notch touches it as shown. At that point, the second petal should curve away from the first petal, and when the appliqué is complete, the petals should not touch beyond the notches. Continue this placement until all petals have been appliquéd.

Due to inconsistency in appliqué stitching, the last petal may not fit exactly in the space remaining. If this occurs, make the necessary adjustment when adding the last petal. If the space is larger than the finished petal, make the petal fit by turning under less seam allowance. If the space is too small, turn under more seam allowance on the sides and make the point shorter.

REVERSE APPLIQUÉ

Reverse, or overlaid, appliqué is a technique in which an upper layer of fabric is turned back to expose a lower layer of fabric. Use reverse appliqué to add detail to rosebuds and tulips, for example.

1. Prepare the upper layer of the fabric as usual for appliqué. Mark the areas where the upper layer will be opened up to expose the lower layer.
2. Cut the lower layer of fabric the exact size of the actual pattern; do not add seam allowances.
3. Layer the upper fabric piece over the lower piece and pin into place. Stitch all around the upper piece as described in needle-turn appliqué instructions on pages 29–31. The lower layer is now encased by the upper layer and is not visible.
4. Separate the upper fabric from the lower piece and carefully cut along the center of the marked area.

Clip sparingly, as needed, toward concave curves.

5. Needle-turn and stitch the turned edges to expose the lower fabric.

LIGHT BOX

Light boxes can be purchased from office or architectural supply stores, but they are expensive. The following is an inexpensive alternative that achieves the same result.

Separate your dining-room table as if adding an extra leaf. Place a piece of glass, plastic, or Plexiglas™ over the opening. Any of these can be purchased from a glass supplier and cut to fit your table, if desired. Be sure to have the glass edges finished, framed, bound, or taped to avoid injury. (I have used the removable glass from a storm door for this purpose.) Set a table lamp on the floor underneath the glass and you have an instant light table.

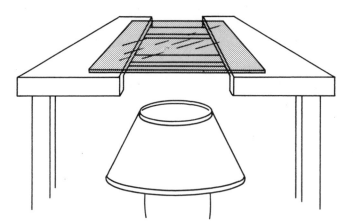

BIBLIOGRAPHY

Bishop, Robert. *New Discoveries in American Quilts*. New York: E. P. Dutton, 1975.

_____. *Quilts, Coverlets, Rugs and Samplers*. New York: Alfred A. Knopf, 1982.

Brackman, Barbara. *American Patchwork Quilt*. Tokyo, Japan: Spencer Museum of Art and Kokusai Art, 1987.

Bresenhan, Karoline Patterson, and Puentes, Nancy O'Bryant. *Lone Stars: A Legacy of Texas Quilts, 1836–1936*. Austin, Texas: University of Texas Press, 1986.

Fox, Sandi. *Small Endearments*. New York: Charles Scribner's Sons, 1985.

Hall, Carrie A., and Kretsinger, Rose G. *The Romance of the Patchwork Quilt in America*. New York: Bonanza Books, 1935.

Havig, Bettina. *Missouri Heritage Quilts*. Paducah, Kentucky: American Quilter's Society, 1986.

Kiracofe, Roderick. "Showcase." *The Quilt Digest* (Vol. 2, 1984), pp. 34–57.

Lasansky, Jeannette. *Pieced By Mother*. Lewisburg, Pennsylvania: Oral Traditions Project of Union County Historical Society, 1987.

MacDowell, Marsha, and Fitzgerald, Ruth D. *Michigan Quilts: 150 Years of a Textile Tradition*. East Lansing, Michigan: Michigan State University Museum, 1987.

Martin, Nancy J., and McCloskey, Marsha. *Ocean Waves*. Bothell, Washington: That Patchwork Place, Inc., 1989.

Nelson, Cyril I. *1983 Quilt Engagement Calendar*.

_____. *1982 Quilt Engagement Calendar*.

Safford, Carleton L., and Bishop, Robert. *America's Quilts & Coverlets*. New York: E. P. Dutton, 1980.

THAT PATCHWORK PLACE PUBLICATIONS

Angelsong by Joan Vibert
Angle Antics by Mary Hickey
Baby Quilts from Grandma by Carolann Palmer
Back to Square One by Nancy J. Martin
A Banner Year by Nancy J. Martin
Basket Garden by Mary Hickey
Blockbuster Quilts by Margaret J. Miller
Cathedral Window: A Fresh Look by Nancy J. Martin
Calendar Quilts by Joan Hanson
Christmas Memories—A Folk Art Celebration
     by Nancy J. Martin
Copy Art for Quilters by Nancy J. Martin
A Dozen Variables by Marsha McCloskey and
     Nancy J. Martin
Even More by Trudie Hughes
Fit To Be Tied by Judy Hopkins
Handmade Quilts by Mimi Dietrich
Happy Endings—Finishing the Edges of Your Quilt
     by Mimi Dietrich
Holiday Happenings by Christal Carter
Home for Christmas by Nancy J. Martin and
     Sharon Stanley
Lessons in Machine Piecing by Marsha McCloskey
Little By Little: Quilts in Miniature by Mary Hickey
More Template-Free™ Quiltmaking by Trudie Hughes
My Mother's Quilts: Designs from the Thirties
     by Sara Nephew
Ocean Waves by Marsha McCloskey and Nancy J. Martin
One-of-a-Kind Quilts by Judy Hopkins
Pieces of the Past by Nancy J. Martin

Pineapple Passion by Nancy Smith and Lynda Milligan
Quilts to Share by Janet Kime
Red and Green: An Appliqué Tradition by Jeana Kimball
Reflections of Baltimore by Jeana Kimball
Scrap Happy by Sally Schneider
Small Quilts by Marsha McCloskey
Small Talk by Donna Lynn Thomas
Stars and Stepping Stones by Marsha McCloskey
Template-Free™ Quiltmaking by Trudie Hughes
Template-Free™ Quilts and Borders by Trudie Hughes
Threads of Time by Nancy J. Martin
Women and Their Quilts by Nancyann Johanson Twelker

Tools
6" Bias Square®
8" Bias Square®
Metric Bias Square®
BiRangle™
Pineapple Rule
Rotary Mate™
Rotary Rule™
ScrapSaver™

Video
Shortcuts to America's
Best-Loved Quilts

Many titles are available at your local quilt shop. For more information, send $2 for a color catalog to That Patchwork Place, Inc., PO Box 118, Bothell WA 98041-0118.